PLAYS FOR PERFORMANCE

*A series designed for
contemporary production and study
Edited by
Nicholas Rudall and Bernard Sahlins*

AUGUST STRINDBERG

The Father

In a New Adaptation by
Robert Brustein

Ivan R. Dee
CHICAGO

Library of Congress Cataloging-in-Publication Data:
Brustein, Robert Sanford, 1927–
    The father / August Strindberg ; in a new adaptation by Robert Brustein.
        p.   cm. — (Plays for performance)
    ISBN 0-929587-87-1 (cloth : alk. paper). —
    ISBN 0-929587-86-3 (paper : alk. paper)
    I. Strindberg, August, 1849–1912. Fadren.   II. Title.
III. Series.
PT9812.F32B78   1992
    839.72'6—dc20
                                            92-8408

INTRODUCTION
by Robert Brustein

August Strindberg's scorching misogynist play *The Father* (1887), would seem to be a risky work for American theatres in the nineties. The playwright was a target for feminists in his own time. He is even more vulnerable today, with his jeremiads against women's desire for dominance in the sexual wars and his appeal to men to reassert their masculine authority ("Wake Hercules, before they take away your club!"). But a careful reading of the play reveals that no matter how feverish or paranoid he seems on the surface, Strindberg manages to anticipate most of the issues arousing women today, particularly the idea that marriage is motivated by politics as much as by romance. The prize in the war between the Captain and Laura is their daughter Bertha, and what must be resolved is which of her parents will determine her future. (Bertha's own desires are scarcely acknowledged.) Laura's chief weapon is to cast doubts on the girl's paternity and her husband's mental stability, doubts which fester in the Captain's brain and eventually drive him to an act of violence that ensures her victory.

The Father, therefore, despite its domestic setting, is a large-scale heroic drama, with two mighty opponents. Its models are not the realistic plays of Henrik Ibsen (an author Strindberg scornfully

3

called "that Norwegian bluestocking"), but rather such classic epics as Aeschylus's *Agamemnon* (another military hero ensnared by a scheming wife) and Kleist's *Pentheselea* with its similar identification of love and war). Strindberg's style, even in his so-called "naturalistic" plays, is essentially distended, contorted, and convulsive. There are large forces at work here, which rattle the walls of the bourgeois drawing room. And the unconscious strains of paranoia, hallucination, even dementia, associated with Expressionist drama, are never far from the surface. It is no wonder that Emile Zola, though he admired *The Father*, could not credit Strindberg's claim that it was an example of the new naturalism. Too much of the work is abstract and undetailed. Most of the characters (the Doctor, the Pastor, even the Captain) are known primarily by generic names. Social environment and biological inheritance are invoked, but only to provide ammunition for the war between the two antagonists. *The Father* is just about as naturalistic as *Othello*, which it also resembles. And that odd passage where the Captain uses Shylock's language in order to claim sympathy for men also suggests that Strindberg owes a considerably greater debt to tragic dramatists like Shakespeare than to any contemporary realists or naturalists.

It is very important, therefore, that productions of *The Father* try to reflect its internal proportions and subjective disturbances. I was convinced of this as long ago as 1949 when, acting off-Broadway in a realistic version of the play, I noticed that the painted flats were shaking from the force of the Captain's fury. In my own production, with Christopher Lloyd and Candy Buckley at the American Repertory Theatre, we tried to cap-

4

ture those convulsive qualities through progressive changes in the decor and acting as the conflict proceeded and the Captain's madness grew. Beginning in the Captain's study, a large room backed with an enormous window and decorated with military materials, hunting trophies, and scientific instruments, the setting looked normal enough at first, except for the final moment of the first act, after the Captain rushes furiously into the snowy night, when a huge image of a marmoset appeared almost subliminally in the background, as a harbinger of feral terrors to come.

In the climactic scene of the second act, when the Captain seals his fate by throwing a lighted lamp at his wife, we had the door through which she escapes burst into flames as the curtain descended. And in the last act, which begins with the Captain feverishly pacing above, his study had undergone a total change, not only seen from an entirely different angle but now claustrophobically enclosed, triangulated, and bathed in an eerie green light. When the Captain finally burst into the room, carrying books in his arms, the door fell noisily into the room, revealing him in a harsh white light, bathed in smoke and dust.

It was at this point that Lloyd's talent for bizarre comic acting was most effectively employed, in such actions as pulling the Pastor's toupee off his head to reveal his alleged cuckold's horns. And the final moment, after the Captain is strapped into a straitjacket and suffers his incapacitating stroke, we staged with Laura hugging Bertha (her trophy), while the Captain revolved slowly on the couch under a special spot, to Philip Glass's mournful haunting music.

One of the most difficult things about directing this play is to find some balance between the two

5

competing antagonists. Laura is depicted as such an unconscionable schemer, and the Captain such an innocent victim, that not only is the battle unequal but it can easily fall into melodrama. Strindberg helps us somewhat by writing those lovely lyrical interludes in which the husband and wife stop fighting for a moment to remember their past together with tenderness and affection (these memories are almost always nonsexual in nature, like a child's relationship to his mother). Usually, however, this Othello is married not to Desdemona but rather to a female Iago, who sows doubts about her own fidelity and his fatherhood of their child in order to destroy the obstacles preventing her complete control of the household.

Strindberg seems undecided about how much of her behavior is conscious. The pastor refers to "an unconscious crime," and Laura herself says that she didn't want "this" to happen (meaning the Captain's defeat at the end). Her remark often makes the audience laugh, since she has obviously worked so hard to make it happen. But for a production to penetrate beneath the melodramatic surface, it must explore and emphasize Laura's positive qualities—her intelligence, her resourcefulness, and, especially, her desperation in a world where men are completely in control of all marital decisions, financial and moral. The first-act scene, when Laura is humiliated over the household accounts, is a good starting place. She must be seen to have no other option, given the unequal laws of the time.

But don't sentimentalize the struggle. Once begun, it is remorseless, inexorable, and unyielding. Unfair as the play is—and the playwright often seems to share his character's paranoia—it is also an unblinkingly honest glimpse into the un-

6

examined motives lurking in many sexual relationships. Strindberg had strong female strains in his own nature. He began his adult life as a feminist. He became a feminist again in his later years. *The Father* shows him trying to repress these qualities but nevertheless focused courageously on one of the subjects that matter most to people today.

Christopher Lloyd and Bronia Stefan Wheeler in the American Repertory Theatre production of *The Father.* (PHOTO BY RICHARD FELDMAN)

CHARACTERS

THE CAPTAIN
THE PASTOR
ORDERLY
NOJD
LAURA
MOTHER-IN-LAW
DR. OSTERMARK
NURSE
BERTHA

The Father

ACT 1

The Captain's office in his house. He is an officer of cavalry in a provincial Swedish town. Shortly before Christmas. In the middle of the room, a large table covered with newspapers, magazines, a large photo album, and a lamp. A leather-covered armchair, sofas, and another smaller table. A writing desk with a pendulum clock on it. Rifles, pistols, and gunbags on the walls. Military tunics hanging on coat stands.

Early evening. The lamp is lighted. The Pastor and the Captain are talking. The Captain is in undress uniform, wearing boots and spurs. The Pastor is in black, with a white cravat in place of his usual clerical collar. The Captain rings. An Orderly enters.

ORDERLY: Yes, sir?

CAPTAIN: Is Nojd out there?

ORDERLY: He's in the kitchen, waiting for orders.

CAPTAIN: In the kitchen again? Call him in!

ORDERLY: Yes, sir. *(he exits)*

PASTOR: What's the problem?

CAPTAIN: Oh, that bastard has knocked up one of the kitchen maids again. He's a thoroughgoing pain in the neck.

PASTOR: Nojd again? Wasn't he in trouble last spring?

13

CAPTAIN: You remember that, do you? Look, do me a favor and have a few words with him. Maybe you can have some influence. I've screamed at him; I've had him flogged. Nothing makes the least impression.

PASTOR: What impression do you think my preaching will have on him? He's a soldier!

CAPTAIN: Well, it's certainly never had any effect on me.

PASTOR: That's true enough.

CAPTAIN: Maybe you'll have more success with him. It's worth a try, anyway. *(enter Nojd, who comes smartly to attention)* So, what have you been up to now, Nojd?

NOJD: Sir, I hope you'll understand, I can't talk about it with the Pastor in the room.

PASTOR: Just pretend I'm not here, lad.

NOJD: Well, sir, it was like this: We were all at a dance at Gabriel's—and then Ludwig said...

CAPTAIN: What the hell does Ludwig have to do with it? Stick to the point, man!

NOJD: Yes, sir. Well, then Emma said she'd like to go into the barn.

CAPTAIN: I see. So it was Emma who seduced *you*.

NOJD: Well, that's not far from it. I mean, nothing happens unless the girl wants it, you know.

CAPTAIN: Look, let's cut out the embroidery. Are you the father of the child or not?

NOJD: How am I supposed to know?

CAPTAIN: What the hell do you mean? You don't *know*?

NOJD: Well, no, sir—you see, nobody can really be sure.

CAPTAIN: You mean there were other men?

NOJD: Not that time, far as I can tell. But you can never be sure.

CAPTAIN: Are you trying to blame Ludwig? Is that your game?

NOJD: It's not easy to say who's to blame.

CAPTAIN: Look, you told Emma you'd marry her, didn't you?

NOJD: Oh, you always have to tell them something like that.

CAPTAIN: *(to the Pastor)* This is dreadful.

PASTOR: It's an old old story. *(to Nojd)* Come on, Nojd, surely you're man enough to admit you're the father.

NOJD: Well, sir, I'll admit I was in the hay with her. But that's not the same thing as being the father. You know that yourself, Pastor.

PASTOR: We're talking about you, lad. Surely you're not going to abandon that girl with an infant child. We can't force you to marry her, but you've got to provide some support for the baby. You *must* do that!

NOJD: Ludwig too, then.

CAPTAIN: We'll have to let the courts decide. I can't get to the bottom of this, and, anyway, it's really none of my business. Get the hell out of here!

PASTOR: One more minute. Nojd, aren't you ashamed to leave that girl destitute with a newborn child? Don't you find that immoral? Don't you?

NOJD: Yes, Pastor, if I really knew the kid was mine. But who can be sure about a thing like that? And who wants to slave all his life for somebody else's brat? You and the Captain can understand that.

CAPTAIN: That's enough, Nojd. Dismissed.

NOJD: Yes, sir, and thank you, sir.

CAPTAIN: And stay the hell out of the kitchen, you bastard. *(Nojd exits)* Well, you certainly weren't a whole lot of help.

PASTOR: What do you mean? I thought I gave him a good talking to.

CAPTAIN: No, you just sat there mumbling to yourself like a maiden aunt.

PASTOR: I have to admit I didn't know what to say. It's tough for the girl, but the lad doesn't have it easy, either. Supposing he isn't the father. The girl nurses the baby for four months at the orphanage and then it gets taken off her hands for good. But a boy can't nurse a child. She can still find a job later on with a decent family, but the boy gets kicked out of the service and his career is ruined.

CAPTAIN: I swear I'd like to be in the courtroom judging this case. Maybe the boy is guilty, there's no way of knowing. But one thing's sure—the girl's responsible, if anyone is.

PASTOR: Well, that's not for me to judge. But what did you want to talk about before this annoying interruption? Bertha's religious training, wasn't it?

CAPTAIN: Not just her religious training, her whole education. This house is bursting with women,

16

all trying to control my child's future. My mother-in-law is teaching her to be a spiritualist; Laura is encouraging her to be an artist; the governess wants her to be a Methodist, old Margaret a Baptist, and the servant girls are recruiting her for the Salvation Army. How do you form a character out of such a crazy quilt? And I, who should have the authority in such a matter, am opposed in all my decisions.

PASTOR: There are too many women running your house.

CAPTAIN: You're right there. It's like putting your head inside a tigers' cage. If I didn't keep a whip under their noses, they'd tear me to pieces. You can well laugh, you scoundrel. First I had to marry your sister, then you dump your step-mother on my doorstep.

PASTOR: Good Lord, I can't have my stepmother living in my house.

CAPTAIN: No, but you don't mind a mother-in-law living in *my* house.

PASTOR: We all have our crosses to bear.

CAPTAIN: Mine's getting just a little too heavy. And then there's my old nurse who still acts like she's changing my diapers. She's a sweet old soul, all right, but I really don't understand what she's doing here.

PASTOR: You really ought to control your women better, Adolph. You give them too much free rein.

CAPTAIN: Oh, so you have some secret formula for controlling women.

17

PASTOR: Well, I will admit that Laura was always difficult to manage, even though she is my sister.

CAPTAIN: Laura has a few faults, it's true. Nothing very serious.

PASTOR: You can speak freely. I know my sister.

CAPTAIN: The romantic notions she was brought up on didn't give her an altogether firm sense of reality. But she is my wife and...

PASTOR: And because she's your wife, she has to be perfect. Come now, my dear brother-in-law, admit that she's your biggest headache.

CAPTAIN: Well, something is turning this household upside down. Laura has made up her mind that Bertha should stay at home, and I've decided she mustn't spend another minute in this madhouse.

PASTOR: So Laura's made up her mind, has she? Then there's going to be difficulties. When she was a child she used to lie on the floor and pretend to be dying until she got her way. Then she'd give back whatever she'd won, saying it wasn't the thing she wanted, anyway, she just wanted her own way.

CAPTAIN: She was the same back then, was she? Hmm. It is true, now that you mention it, that she sometimes makes herself so upset I get worried about her health.

PASTOR: What's your disagreement over Bertha? Are you so far apart that you can't reach a compromise?

CAPTAIN: Don't get the idea I want Bertha to be special—or a carbon copy of myself. But I refuse to throw her into the marriage market, like

18

some pimp soliciting customers. What if she didn't find a husband? She'd have a miserable time of it. But neither do I want to see her stuck with some useless male career if she *did* marry.

PASTOR: So what *do* you want?

CAPTAIN: I want her to be a teacher. That way she could support herself is she stayed single—at least as well as those poor schoolmasters who have to carry an entire family on their salary. And if she did finally marry, she'd be in a position to educate her children. Doesn't that make sense?

PASTOR: It's reasonable—but what about her talent? Isn't it wrong to suppress her artistic gifts?

CAPTAIN: No, I showed her work to a reputable painter, who said it was nothing more than schoolgirl stuff. But then, last summer, some young smartass came along who knew a lot better, of course, and told her she was a genius, so it all turned out the way Laura wanted it.

PASTOR: Was he in love with Bertha?

CAPTAIN: What do you think?

PASTOR: Well, God help you, my friend, you're in for a lot of trouble. The whole thing must be extremely tiresome for you, and I suppose Laura has her allies (*indicating other rooms*)... in there.

CAPTAIN: That's certain. This entire household is at war, and just between you and me, they're not exactly up on the laws of chivalry.

PASTOR: (*rising*) You think I don't know that?

CAPTAIN: You do?

19

PASTOR: Of course.

CAPTAIN: The worst thing is that Bertha's life might be determined by hateful ideas. All they talk about is how men must realize that women can do this and women can do that. It's Man versus Woman all day long. Do you have to go already? Please stay for supper. I don't know what we're having, but stay anyway. You know I'm expecting the new doctor. Have you met him yet?

PASTOR: I got a look at him on my way out here. He seems perfectly pleasant and decent.

CAPTAIN: Well, that's good. Do you think he'll be an ally? My ally, I mean?

PASTOR: Who knows? It all depends on how much experience he's had with women.

CAPTAIN: So you won't stay?

PASTOR: No, thank you, my friend. I promised to be home this evening, and my wife gets disturbed if I'm late.

CAPTAIN: Disturbed? Infuriated, you mean. Well, do what you have to. Let me help you with your coat.

PASTOR: It's certainly very cold tonight. Thanks a lot. You ought to watch your health, Adolph. You seem a little edgy.

CAPTAIN: Edgy? I do?

PASTOR: Yes. I'm not sure you're completely well.

CAPTAIN: Who put that idea in your head? Laura? For the last twenty years she's been treating me like I was on the point of death.

PASTOR: Laura? No. But I'm worried about you.

Watch out for yourself, that's my advice. Well, goodbye, dear friend. Unless you want to settle this business about Bertha's confirmation.

CAPTAIN: Forget about it. The whole thing will take its inevitable course in keeping with the official conscience. I have no intention of being a witness to the faith or a martyr. Those days are over. Goodbye, and regards to your wife.

PASTOR: And love to Laura, Adolph. Goodbye. *(he leaves)*

(the Captain goes to his desk and starts to work on the accounts)

CAPTAIN: Thirty-four—plus nine is forty-three—seven, eight, makes fifty-eight...

LAURA: *(entering from the next room)* Would you please...

CAPTAIN: Just a minute! Fifty-eight...seventy-one, eighty-four, eighty-nine, ninety-two, a hundred. What is it?

LAURA: Am I disturbing you?

CAPTAIN: Not a bit. The housekeeping money?

LAURA: Yes, the housekeeping money.

CAPTAIN: Put the itemized receipts on the desk and I'll go over them.

LAURA: Receipts?

CAPTAIN: Yes.

LAURA: Am I supposed to keep accounts now?

CAPTAIN: Of course you're supposed to keep accounts. We're having serious money problems. If I have to declare bankruptcy, they'll need the proper documentation. Otherwise we can be accused of fraud.

LAURA: It's not my fault that you're having money problems.

CAPTAIN: That's what the accounts will show.

LAURA: It's not my fault your tenant doesn't pay his rent.

CAPTAIN: Who suggested him in the first place? You! And why did you recommend such a notorious freeloader?

LAURA: If you thought he was a freeloader, why did you take him on?

CAPTAIN: Because I wasn't allowed to eat or sleep or work in peace until you got him here. You liked him because your brother didn't; your mother liked him because *I* didn't; the governess liked him because he was a Methodist, and old Margaret liked him because she had known his grandmother since childhood. You want to know why I took him? That's why! And if I hadn't taken him, I'd either be in an insane asylum by now or in the family crypt. Anyhow, here's the housekeeping money and your allowance. You can give me the receipts later.

LAURA: *(makes an ironic curtsy)* Thank you very much. And you—do you keep receipts for everything you spend—outside the household?

CAPTAIN: That's none of your business.

LAURA: Of course not. Just as my child's education is none of my business. So, did you gentlemen reach any agreement at your conference tonight?

CAPTAIN: I had already made my decision. I just

wanted a chance to tell it to my one friend in the family. Bertha will live in town. She leaves in two weeks.

LAURA: And where exactly will she live?

CAPTAIN: With Mr. Savberg, the lawyer.

LAURA: Savberg! That Freethinker!

CAPTAIN: According to the law as it's presently written, children are brought up in their father's faith.

LAURA: And the mother has nothing to say?

CAPTAIN: Not a thing. She gives up all legal rights to her husband. In return, he must agree to support her and her children.

LAURA: She has no rights over her own child?

CAPTAIN: None at all. When you sell something, you can't get it back and keep the money, too.

LAURA: What if the mother and father agree to a compromise?

CAPTAIN: What compromise? I want her to live in town, you want her to live home. If we compromised, she'd be living in the railway station, halfway between town and home. You see? It's a deadlock.

LAURA: Then the lock must be broken.... What was Nojd doing here?

CAPTAIN: That's a professional secret.

LAURA: Which the whole kitchen knows.

CAPTAIN: Then you know, too.

LAURA: Of course.

CAPTAIN: And you're all ready to hand down your judgment of guilt.

LAURA: That's for the law to do.

CAPTAIN: The law can't determine who the child's father is.

LAURA: People can tell that.

CAPTAIN: Intelligent people believe you can never tell that.

LAURA: Remarkable! You can't know who the child's father is?

CAPTAIN: So I'm told.

LAURA: Quite remarkable. Then how can a father hold any rights over a mother's child?

CAPTAIN: He holds them because he's taken on responsibility for the child—or been forced to take it on. In marriage, of course, paternity is not subject to doubt.

LAURA: Not subject to doubt?

CAPTAIN: I should hope not.

LAURA: But suppose the wife has been unfaithful.

CAPTAIN: Well, conjecture of that kind is not relevant to this issue. Is there anything else you want to discuss?

LAURA: No, nothing else.

CAPTAIN: Then I'm going up to my room. Please let me know when the doctor comes. *(closes the desk drawer and rises)*

LAURA: I will.

CAPTAIN: *(going out the door)* The moment he comes, understand? I don't want to be rude. *(exit)*

LAURA: I understand. *(she looks at the money in her hand)*

MOTHER-IN-LAW: *(offstage)* Laura!

LAURA: Yes, Mama.

MOTHER-IN-LAW: Is my tea ready yet?

LAURA: *(at the door of the next room)* It'll be ready in a minute. *(the Orderly opens the hall door)*

ORDERLY: Dr. Ostermark.

(Enter Doctor. Exit Orderly, closing the door.)

LAURA: *(shaking hands)* How do you do, Dr. Ostermark? Welcome to our house. I'm afraid the Captain has gone out, but he'll be back soon.

DOCTOR: I want to apologize for calling on you so late, but I had to make a number of calls on the way.

LAURA: Please sit down.

DOCTOR: Thank you.

LAURA: Yes, there is a lot of illness around these days, but I hope you'll like the place anyway. It's very important in a lonely province like ours to have a doctor who takes some interest in his patients. People speak very well of you, Dr. Ostermark. I hope we can be friends.

DOCTOR: You are very kind, dear lady. But I trust my visits here will not be professional ones. I assume your family is generally in good health, and that...

LAURA: Yes, the family's been lucky enough to avoid any serious illness, but still...things are not exactly what they should be.

DOCTOR: Yes?

25

LAURA: No, I'm afraid things are not at all what they should be.

DOCTOR: My, my, you worry me.

LAURA: There are always secrets in family life that one has to keep hidden from the outside world.

DOCTOR: But not from your doctor.

LAURA: No. And that's why it's necessary to tell you everything right away.

DOCTOR: Don't you think we could postpone this talk until I've had a chance to meet the Captain?

LAURA: No. We have to talk before you meet him.

DOCTOR: It has to do with him, then?

LAURA: Yes, him. My poor, dear husband.

DOCTOR: This is very disturbing. Whatever the problem is, I hope you know you can confide in me.

LAURA: *(taking out her handkerchief)* My husband's mind is going. There, I've told you, and later you can judge for yourself.

DOCTOR: I'm astonished. I'm a great admirer of the Captain's scholarly work on mineralogy. It is the product of a clear and powerful intellect.

LAURA: Is it? I would be so happy if we—his relatives—could be proven wrong.

DOCTOR: It's entirely possible, of course, that his mind has been affected in other ways. Tell me . . .

LAURA: That's exactly what we fear. You see, there are times when he gets the most peculiar ideas. You could forgive that in a scientist, if it weren't such a problem for his family. For example, he has an absolute mania about buying things.

DOCTOR: That's interesting. What sort of things?

LAURA: Books. He buys cartons and cartons of them, which he never reads.

DOCTOR: It's not unusual for a scholar to buy books.

LAURA: You don't believe what I'm saying?

DOCTOR: I believe you believe what you're saying, madam.

LAURA: Tell me this. Can someone see what is happening on another planet through a microscope?

DOCTOR: He says he can do that?

LAURA: That's exactly what he says.

DOCTOR: Through a microscope?

LAURA: A microscope. Yes.

DOCTOR: That is significant, yes, if it's true.

LAURA: If it's true? I see you don't believe me, Doctor. So I'm forced to let you in on a closely guarded family secret.

DOCTOR: My dear lady, I am honored by your confidences, but I'm a doctor. I must do an examination before giving a diagnosis. Does the Captain show any evidence of instability, any lack of will power?

LAURA: Does he! We've been married for twenty years now, and he's never made a decision he hasn't reversed.

DOCTOR: Is he dogmatic?

LAURA: Well, he always insists on having his way, but as soon as he gets it, he loses interest and makes me decide on everything.

DOCTOR: That's an important piece of evidence. The will, you see, madam, is the backbone of the mind. If it shatters, the mind shatters, too.

LAURA: God knows, I've tried my best to please him during these difficult years. Oh, if you only knew what I've gone through with him, if you only knew!

DOCTOR: I'm very upset to hear of your troubles, madam, and I promise I'll do what I can. You know you can count on my sympathy and help. But I must ask for something in return. Don't ever permit anything to prey on the patient's mind. When the will is unstable, an idea can take hold and become an obsession. That's how people grow into paranoiacs. Do you understand?

LAURA: . . . You mean I shouldn't let him get ideas into his head.

DOCTOR: Exactly. A sick man can be made to believe anything. He is especially open to suggestion.

LAURA: I see . . . I understand. Yes, yes. *(a bell rings within)* Excuse me a moment. That's my mother's ring. . . . Oh, here's Adolph.

(Laura exits and the Captain enters)

CAPTAIN: So you've arrived, Doctor. Welcome to our house.

DOCTOR: I'm very glad to meet you, Captain. It's a great honor to shake the hand of such a distinguished scientist.

CAPTAIN: Oh, please. But unfortunately, my duties as a military man don't give me much time for research. . . . Still, I believe I'm on the verge of a really striking discovery.

28

DOCTOR: Is that so?

CAPTAIN: I've been doing a spectrum analysis on some meteoric stones, and I've turned up carbon—which suggests the existence of organic life. What do you think of that?

DOCTOR: And you can see that through a microscope?

CAPTAIN: No, for God's sake, a *spectroscope*!

DOCTOR: A spectroscope! Forgive me. Then that means that you'll soon be able to tell us what's happening on Jupiter.

CAPTAIN: Not what is happening—what's already happened. If only that goddamned bookseller in Paris would send me the books I ordered. I'm beginning to think the whole publishing trade is conspiring against me. Look, for two months I haven't had a single reply to my orders, my letters, or my abusive telegrams. It's driving me crazy! I can't understand what's wrong.

DOCTOR: Just the normal inefficiency. Don't let it upset you so much.

CAPTAIN: Yes, but the hell of it is that I won't meet the deadline on my article—I know for certain they're doing the same experiments in Berlin. ...Anyway, we shouldn't be talking about that, but about you. If you want to live here, we have a small suite of rooms in the other wing. Or maybe you'd like to live in your predecessor's quarters?

DOCTOR: Whatever you choose.

CAPTAIN: No, whatever *you* choose. It's for you to say.

29

DOCTOR: You decide, Captain.

CAPTAIN: Absolutely not. You have to decide which you prefer. I don't care one way or the other.

DOCTOR: I really don't think I can....

CAPTAIN: For Chrissake, man, say what you want! I have no will in this matter, no desire, no opinion. Are you such a weakling that you can't make up your own mind? Make a decision or I'll lose my temper.

DOCTOR: If it's up to me, I'd rather live here.

CAPTAIN: Good! Thank you. *(rings)* I'm sorry, Doctor, forgive me, but nothing makes me angrier than indecisive people. *(enter the Nurse)* Ah, Margaret. Listen, my dear, do you know if the rooms in the wing are ready for the Doctor?

NURSE: Yes, Captain, they're all made up.

CAPTAIN: Good. Then I won't hold you up any longer, Doctor. You must be worn out. Good night—and once again, welcome to our house. I hope to see you in the morning.

DOCTOR: Thank you. Good night.

CAPTAIN: By the way, did my wife fill you in at all about the way things are here?

DOCTOR: Your good wife did mention one or two items she thought it might be wise for a stranger to know. Good night again, Captain.

(the Nurse shows the Doctor out and returns)

CAPTAIN: What's up, old girl? Anything wrong?

NURSE: Now you listen to me, Mr. Adolph, dear.

30

CAPTAIN: Go on and talk, Margaret. You're the only one who doesn't get on my nerves.

NURSE: Then listen, Mr. Adolph. Can't you let the Madam have her way a little in this business over the child? Think about the mother....

CAPTAIN: Think about the father, Margaret.

NURSE: Now, now, now! A father has a lot of things, but the mother only has her child.

CAPTAIN: That's true, my girl. She has only one responsibility while I have three and hers as well. Do you think I'd have been stuck in this army job all my life if I didn't have to support her and her child?

NURSE: I know, I know—but that's not what I wanted to talk to you about.

CAPTAIN: I agree. What you want to talk to me about was how I'm in the wrong.

NURSE: Don't you believe I want the best for you, Mr. Adolph?

CAPTAIN: I'm sure you do, old dear, but you don't know what's best for me. You see, I'm not satisfied just to give my child life. I want to give her my soul.

NURSE: That's too deep for me. I just think you two should be able to agree.

CAPTAIN: You are not my friend, Margaret.

NURSE: Not your friend?! Me? My God, how can you say that, Mr. Adolph? Can you ever forget that I held you in my arms when you were a baby?

CAPTAIN: How can I forget that, my dear?

You've always been like a mother to me, and you've always stood by me. But now when I really need you, you desert the camp and join the enemy.

NURSE: Enemy?

CAPTAIN: Yes, enemy. You know how things are here. You've watched it from the beginning.

NURSE: Ah, I've seen plenty. But, dear God, why do two people torture each other so? People who are so good and kind to everyone else? The Madam never treats me badly or...

CAPTAIN: Only me, I know. I'm telling you, Margaret, if you desert me now, you'll be doing something evil. For a net is closing around me, and that doctor is not my friend.

NURSE: Dear God, Mr. Adolph, you think the worst of everyone. But that's because you're not a believer in the true faith. That's your problem.

CAPTAIN: And you and the other Baptists have found the true faith, right? That must make you happy.

NURSE: I'm happier than you are, Mr. Adolph. Humble your proud heart and God will bless you in your love for your neighbor.

CAPTAIN: Isn't it odd, but every time you mention God and love, your voice gets hard and your eyes turn dark. No, Margaret, you haven't found the true faith.

NURSE: Yes, you're proud and you know a lot about books, but that won't help when it comes to the Day of Judgment.

CAPTAIN: How arrogantly you speak, humble heart!

32

I'm fully aware that learning means nothing to creatures like you.

NURSE: Shame on you for that! Still, your old Margaret still loves her great big boy the best. And when troubles come, he'll come back to her, like a good child.

CAPTAIN: Forgive me, Margaret. You really are the only friend I have. Help me, something is about to happen. I don't know what, but I know it's awful, this evil thing that's on the way. *(a scream from within)* What's that! Who's screaming? *(Bertha runs in)*

BERTHA: Papa, Papa! Help me! Save me!

CAPTAIN: What's the matter? Tell me, darling.

BERTHA: Protect me! I know she's going to do something awful to me.

CAPTAIN: Who? What are you talking about? Tell me.

BERTHA: It's Grandma. But it was my fault. I lied to her.

CAPTAIN: Go on.

BERTHA: I will. But you won't tell anyone, will you? Promise me.

CAPTAIN: I promise. But tell me what happened. *(exit Nurse)*

BERTHA: Sometimes, in the evening, she turns down the lamp and makes me sit at a table and hold a pen over a piece of paper. She says the spirits will write.

CAPTAIN: Well, I'll be damned. And you never told me.

BERTHA: I didn't dare. Grandma says the spirits will punish anyone who mentions them. And then the pen starts writing, and I don't know if I'm doing it or not. Sometimes it goes the way it's supposed to, but sometimes nothing happens at all. When I'm tired it doesn't work, but I have to make it work anyway. Tonight I thought it was going all right, but then Grandma said it was all out of a book and I was playing a trick on her. And she really got angry.

CAPTAIN: Do you believe in spirits?

BERTHA: I'm not sure.

CAPTAIN: But *I'm* sure they don't exist.

BERTHA: Grandma says you don't know about these things, and that you have evil instruments that can look into other planets.

CAPTAIN: She says that, does she? What else does she say?

BERTHA: She says you can't work miracles.

CAPTAIN: I never said I could. Do you know anything about meteorites? Stones that fall from other stars? Well, I analyze these to learn if they contain the same elements as Earth. That's all I do.

BERTHA: Grandma says she can see things that you can't.

CAPTAIN: My dear, she's lying.

BERTHA: Grandma never lies.

CAPTAIN: How do you know that?

BERTHA: Then Mother lies too.

CAPTAIN: Hm!

34

BERTHA: If you call Mother a liar, I'll never believe another word you say.

CAPTAIN: I never said that, so you must believe me. This above all, that your happiness, your future, depends entirely on your leaving home. Will you do this? Will you live in town where you can learn something useful?

BERTHA: Oh yes, I'd love to live in town—anywhere but here! As long as I can still see you. It's always so gloomy in there, like a winter's night. But when you come home, Father, it's like a morning in spring, when they take down the storm windows and the light comes through.

CAPTAIN: My darling, darling child.

BERTHA: But you must be good to Mother. She cries so much.

CAPTAIN: Hm!...So you prefer to live in town.

BERTHA: Oh yes!

CAPTAIN: Even if your mother doesn't want you to go?

BERTHA: She must.

CAPTAIN: But what if she doesn't?

BERTHA: Then I don't know. But she must! She must!

CAPTAIN: Will you ask her?

BERTHA: You ask her—but do it very nicely. She won't listen to me.

CAPTAIN: Hm!...Well, if you want it, and I want it, and she doesn't, what should we do then.

BERTHA: Oh, then the fights will start all over again. Why can't you both...*(enter Laura)*

35

LAURA: So you're in here, Bertha. Well, Adolph, since we still haven't decided on her future, let's hear what *she* has to say.

CAPTAIN: Bertha is hardly an expert on the development of young girls. But you and I have watched enough grow up to know what we're talking about.

LAURA: But we don't agree. Bertha can cast the deciding vote.

CAPTAIN: No. I won't let anyone usurp my rights—not a woman, and not a child. Bertha, I think you should leave.

(exit Bertha)

LAURA: You were scared to hear her opinion because you knew she would agree with me.

CAPTAIN: As a matter of fact, I know she wants to leave home. But I also know you have the power to change her mind.

LAURA: Do I have so much power?

CAPTAIN: Yes, you have a diabolical power—like all ruthless people who don't care how they get their way. How did you get rid of Doctor Nordling, for example? And how did you get the new man here?

LAURA: Yes, how did I?

CAPTAIN: You undermined Nordling until he couldn't stand it here anymore, and then you convinced your brother to put the pressure on for this one.

LAURA: Nothing unlawful about that, is there? So Bertha is going to leave home?

CAPTAIN: In two weeks.

LAURA: You should know I'll do my best to stop it.

CAPTAIN: You can't.

LAURA: I can't? Do you expect me to turn my child over to godless people who'll tell her everything she's learned from me is nonsense? She would despise me for the rest of my life.

CAPTAIN: Do you expect me to let ignorant, arrogant women teach my daughter that her father is a fake?

LAURA: That shouldn't worry you—now.

CAPTAIN: What the hell do you mean?

LAURA: I mean the mother is closer to the child. You said yourself that no one can tell who the father is.

CAPTAIN: How does that apply to us?

LAURA: You don't know if you are Bertha's father.

CAPTAIN: I don't know?

LAURA: How can you know when nobody knows?

CAPTAIN: You are joking.

LAURA: No, I'm just trying out your own theory. How do you know I haven't been unfaithful?

CAPTAIN: I can believe a lot about you, but not that. Even if it were true, you would hardly admit it to me.

LAURA: Suppose I was prepared for anything— to be rejected, ridiculed, kicked out of the house —anything to keep control of my child. Suppose I am telling the truth when I tell you that Bertha is my child, but not yours. Suppose...

37

CAPTAIN: Stop it!!

LAURA: Just suppose...your power would be over.

CAPTAIN: Not until you could prove I wasn't the father.

LAURA: Is that so difficult? Is that what you want?

CAPTAIN: Stop.

LAURA: All I need to do is name the real father—citing details of time and place, of course. Let's see. When was Bertha born? We'd been married three years...

CAPTAIN: If you don't stop, I'll...

LAURA: You'll what? All right, we'll stop. But you'd better think twice before making any more decisions. You don't want to appear ridiculous.

CAPTAIN: I find this whole thing very sad.

LAURA: Which makes you even more ridiculous.

CAPTAIN: But not you?

LAURA: Women are much too clever.

CAPTAIN: That's why men can't fight you.

LAURA: Why fight a superior enemy?

CAPTAIN: Superior?

LAURA: Yes. I don't know why, but I've never been able to look at a man without feeling superior to him.

CAPTAIN: One day you will meet your superior. And you won't forget it.

LAURA: That will be interesting.

(enter Nurse)

38

NURSE: Dinner's ready. Please come to the table.

LAURA: Yes, of course. *(the Captain hangs back, and sits down in a chair near the sofa)* Are you coming?

CAPTAIN: No, thanks, I don't want anything to eat.

LAURA: Why not? You're upset.

CAPTAIN: No, I'm just not hungry.

LAURA: Please come or they'll start asking questions, and we don't want that. Try to be sensible. No? You won't? All right, stay there then. *(exit)*

NURSE: Mr. Adolph, what's happening now?

CAPTAIN: I'm not sure yet. Tell me, why do you women treat grown men like babies?

NURSE: For goodness sake, you're all our children, aren't you? All men, big and small....

CAPTAIN: But no man gives birth to a woman, is that what you mean? True. But I must be the father of Bertha. You believe that, Margaret, don't you? Don't you?

NURSE: Lord sake, you are a silly boy. Of course you're the father of your child. Now come and eat. Don't sit around sulking. There, there, come along.

CAPTAIN: *(rising)* Get the hell out, woman. To hell with hags. *(at the hall door)* Svard! Svard!

ORDERLY: *(entering)* Yes, sir?

CAPTAIN: Tie up the horses to the covered sleigh. At once!

(exit Orderly)

NURSE: Listen to me, Captain....

39

CAPTAIN: Get the hell out, woman. *Out!*

NURSE: God help us, what's going to happen now?

CAPTAIN: *(putting on his cap)* I won't be home before midnight. *(exit)*

NURSE: Lord Jesus! What's going to happen now.

(thunder and lightning...blackout)

ACT 2

The same. Late that night. Doctor and Laura talking.

DOCTOR: After my talk with him, I find your suspicions may be without foundation. For one
thing, you were wrong to say he had made his
astonishing discoveries with a microscope. Ap-
parently, it was a spectroscope. This not only
suggests that his mind is sound but that he
has made a great contribution to scientific
knowledge.

LAURA: I never said that.

DOCTOR: I made notes of our conversation, madam,
and I remember questioning you very closely on
this point because I thought I had heard wrong.
One has to be absolutely precise about charges
that might lead to a man being committed.

LAURA: Committed?

DOCTOR: I assume you know that when someone is
certified insane, he loses all civil and family
rights.

LAURA: No, I was not aware of that.

DOCTOR: I'd like to clear up one more dubious
point. He said he hadn't been receiving any
response from his booksellers. May I ask you—
and I don't question your good intentions—have
you been intercepting his letters?

LAURA: Yes. I have a duty to protect my household. I can't stand by and let him ruin us all.

DOCTOR: I'm sorry, but I don't think you've properly weighed the consequences of your actions. If he discovers you've been secretly interfering in his business, his suspicions will be aroused and paranoia may develop. By thwarting his will, you have already driven him near the edge. I'm sure you know how maddening it is to have your strongest wishes blocked.

LAURA: I'm sure I do.

DOCTOR: Then consider how he feels!

LAURA: *(Clock tolls. Laura rises.)* It's midnight and he's still not home. Now we can expect the worst.

DOCTOR: Tell me what happened the night I left. It's important for me to know everything.

LAURA: He raved on and on about the wildest things. Can you believe he suspects that he is not the father of his own child?

DOCTOR: That is very strange. How did he get such an idea in his head?

LAURA: I really don't know—perhaps from a child support hearing he had with one of his men. When I spoke up for the girl, he got all excited and said no one could tell who a child's father was. I did everything I could to calm him, God knows, but I don't think anything can help him now. *(weeps)*

DOCTOR: This can't go on. Something must be done —but without arousing his suspicions. Tell me this: Has the Captain ever displayed such delusions before?

LAURA: Six years ago, things were much the same, and then he actually confessed—in a letter to his doctor—that he feared for his reason.

DOCTOR: This is clearly a deep-rooted problem, but the sanctity of family life...and so forth...I musn't go too deep or inquire too far. What is done cannot be undone, unfortunately. Yet there must be a remedy linked to the past.... Where do you think he is now?

LAURA: I have no idea. He has such wild notions these days....

DOCTOR: Do you want me to stay until he returns? I could say—well, that your mother is sick and I came by to see her.

LAURA: Yes, tell him that. Please stand by us, Doctor. You have no idea how nervous I am. But wouldn't it be better to tell him what you think of his condition?

DOCTOR: We don't do that unless the patient mentions it himself, and rarely then. A lot depends on the way the case evolves. But we shouldn't stay here. Maybe I should go into the next room. It might look more natural.

LAURA: Yes, that would look better, and Margaret can come in here. She usually waits up for him, and she's the only one with any influence. *(at the door)* Margaret! Margaret!

(enter the Nurse)

NURSE: Did you call me, madam? Is the master back yet?

LAURA: No, but you can sit here and wait for him. When he comes, say my mother is sick and the doctor is in there with her.

43

NURSE: Yes, madam, I'll take care of things.

LAURA: *(going into the inner room)* Will you come with me, Doctor?

DOCTOR: Yes, thank you.

(They leave. The Nurse sits down and picks up her hymnal and glasses.)

NURSE: *(reading half-aloud)* Ah me, ah me.

> How sorrowful, how sad a thing
> Is life's swift journey by.
> Death passes on an angel's wing,
> Above our vale of sighs:
> 'Tis vanity, all vanity.
> Yes, yes! Ah yes!
> Everything that draws a breath
> Is harrowed by his scythe.
> And sorrow only, spared by death,
> Survives the passing life.
> 'Tis vanity, all vanity!
> Yes, yes.

(Bertha enters with a coffeepot and embroidery. She speaks low.)

BERTHA: Can I sit with you, Margaret? It's so lonely in there.

NURSE: My heavens! Bertha, are you still awake?

BERTHA: I have to work on Father's present for Christmas. And I've brought a little something for you.

NURSE: But, dear heart, this won't do. You have to get up early in the morning and it's past midnight now.

BERTHA: That doesn't matter. I can't stay up there alone. I hear ghosts.

44

NURSE: There now, didn't I say so? This is not a good house, mark my words. What did you hear, Bertha?

BERTHA: Maybe it was my imagination, but I heard someone singing in the attic.

NURSE: In the attic? At this time of night?

BERTHA: Yes, and it was such a sad song, the saddest I ever heard. And it seemed to come from the room where the cradle is—you know, the one on the left.

NURSE: Oh dear, oh dear! And it's such a terrible night, too. I think the chimneys will blow down. "Ah, but this earthly life is torn / With sorrow, pain, and grief forlorn / And even when our lives seem fair / 'Tis vanity that triumphs there." Oh, dear child, may God send us a happy Christmas.

BERTHA: Margaret, it is true that Papa is sick?

NURSE: Yes, it's true.

BERTHA: Then we won't have a party Christmas eve. Why isn't he in bed if he's sick?

NURSE: Well, my dearest one, bed doesn't help his kind of sickness. Shh, someone's outside. Go to bed now—and take the coffeepot with you, or your father will be angry.

BERTHA: *(going out with the pot)* Good night, Margaret.

NURSE: Good night, my dear one, and may God bless you.

(enter the Captain)

45

CAPTAIN: *(taking off his greatcoat)* You still up, Margaret? Go to bed!

NURSE: I was only waiting until... *(Captain lights a candle, opens his desk, sits down at it, takes letters and newspapers out of his pocket)* Mr. Adolph...

CAPTAIN: What is it?

NURSE: Old mistress is sick. The doctor is here.

CAPTAIN: Anything serious?

NURSE: No, I don't think so. A little touch of the chills.

CAPTAIN: *(rising)* Who was the father of your child, Margaret?

NURSE: Oh, I've told you that many times. It was that scoundrel Johansson.

CAPTAIN: Are you sure?

NURSE: Don't be a baby. Of course I'm sure, since he was the only one.

CAPTAIN: Ah yes, but was he sure he was the only one? How could he be sure? Only you could be sure. You see? There's the difference.

NURSE: I don't see the difference.

CAPTAIN: No, you don't see it—but it's there all the same. *(turns over a photograph on the desk)* Do you think Bertha favors me?

NURSE: You're like peas in a pod.

CAPTAIN: Did Johansson admit he was the father?

NURSE: He had to.

CAPTAIN: Dreadful. Dreadful. Ah, here's the doc-

46

tor. *(enter the Doctor)* Good evening, Doctor, and how is my mother-in-law feeling?

DOCTOR: Nothing serious. Just a sprained ankle.

CAPTAIN: But Margaret said it was a chill. Your diagnoses don't seem to agree. Margaret, go to bed. *(Exit Nurse. Pause.)* Please sit down, Doctor Ostermark.

DOCTOR: *(sitting)* Thank you.

CAPTAIN: Is it true that if you breed a mare with a zebra the foals are striped?

DOCTOR: *(astonished)* That's quite true.

CAPTAIN: And therefore under certain conditions a stallion can sire striped foals?

DOCTOR: That is also true.

CAPTAIN: So the fact that an offspring resembles its father is proof of nothing.

DOCTOR: Oh...

CAPTAIN: In short, paternity cannot be proven.

DOCTOR: Hm...Well...

CAPTAIN: You're a widower, aren't you? Any children?

DOCTOR: Ye-es.

CAPTAIN: Didn't you ever feel ridiculous as a father? I know of nothing more absurd than to see a man holding his child's hand in the street and referring to "My children." What he ought to say is "My wife's children." Didn't you ever feel how fake your position was? Weren't you ever bothered by doubts—I won't say "suspi-

47

cions," since, as a gentleman, I must assume your wife was above suspicion.

DOCTOR: No I was not. And Captain, wasn't it Goethe who said a man must take his children on trust?

CAPTAIN: Trust? With a woman in the picture? A bit risky, isn't it?

DOCTOR: Oh! There are many different kinds of women.

CAPTAIN: Modern science has proved there's only one!... When I was young and, if I may say, not bad-looking, I had two encounters that are relevant to this discussion. The first took place on a cruise ship. I was sitting in the saloon with some friends when a young stewardess ran in, flung herself down near me, burst into tears, and told us that her sweetheart had drowned. We sympathized with her and I ordered champagne. After the second glass, I touched her foot, after the fourth her knee, and by morning I had... consoled her.

DOCTOR: One swallow doesn't make a summer.

CAPTAIN: You want a summer swallow? Here's the second encounter. I was spending the summer in Lysenkil where I got to know a young woman who was there with her children—her husband was away. She was religious, idealistic, ready with moral lectures, entirely virtuous—or so I thought. I lent her some books and was surprised when she returned them. Three months later, I found her card in one of those books, along with an open declaration of love. It was innocent—as innocent as such a declaration could be from a married woman to a man who

48

never made a move towards her. Now comes the moral. Don't believe too much in anyone.

DOCTOR: Or too little either.

CAPTAIN: Everything in moderation, eh, Doctor? But you see, this woman was so unconsciously dishonest she even told her husband about her feelings. That's what's so dangerous. Women's duplicity is entirely unconscious. That fact softens my judgment. It doesn't change it.

DOCTOR: Your thinking seems to be taking a morbid turn. You ought to watch it.

CAPTAIN: Morbid? I don't think so. Look, Doctor, all steam boilers explode when the pressure gets high enough, but the limit is different for every boiler. Got it? Meanwhile, I know you're here to keep an eye on me. If I weren't a man, I could whine and snivel and ask you to understand my problems, including my past history. But having the misfortune to be a man, I must, like the Roman stoic, fold my arms across my breast and hold my breath until I die. Good night.

DOCTOR: If you are ill, Captain, it doesn't demean your manhood to talk to me about it. In fact, it is my duty to hear both sides of the case.

CAPTAIN: I suspect you can be satisfied with just the one.

DOCTOR: That's wrong. And let me tell you, Captain, when I heard Mrs. Alving talking about her dead husband, I thought what a damned shame the fellow was dead.

CAPTAIN: Do you think he'd have spoken up if he'd been alive? Do you think any dead husband would be believed if he came back to life? Good

49

night, Doctor. You can see I'm perfectly calm. It's safe for you to go to bed.

DOCTOR: Good night then, Captain. I'm withdrawing from the case.

CAPTAIN: Then we're enemies?

DOCTOR: Far from it. I just find it a pity that we can't be friends. Good night. (*Exit. The Captain shows the Doctor out the hall door in back, then crosses to the hall door and opens it.*)

CAPTAIN: Come in. We need to talk. I know you were out there eavesdropping. (*Enter Laura, embarrassed. The Captain sits at his desk.*) It's late, but we have to have things out. Sit down. (*she sits*) This time *I* went to the post office to pick up the mail. This correspondence makes it clear that you have been intercepting my letters—both incoming and outgoing. The result is a loss of irreplaceable time for the completion of my work.

LAURA: My intentions were good. You were neglecting your duties for unnecessary affairs.

CAPTAIN: Hardly good intentions. You knew perfectly well that I would soon gain more distinction from my research than from my military duties. You wanted to block my fame because it would only heighten your own insignificance. In retaliation, I have intercepted letters of yours.

LAURA: One of your nobler actions.

CAPTAIN: I'm aware of your high opinion of me. From these letters, it appears that for a period of time you have been alienating my former friends by spreading rumors about my mental condition. You've been successful. Now there's hardly a person from the Colonel down to the cook who believes in my sanity. The facts of my condition are these: My reason is unaffected, as you know, so I can still fulfill my duties as a soldier and a father. My emotions are fairly well under control, at least as long as my will power holds. But you have so battered away at my emotions that the whole mechanism can collapse at any moment and break into pieces. I won't appeal to your feelings. You have none. That is your strength. Let me appeal to your self-interest.

LAURA: Go on.

CAPTAIN: You behavior has made me so suspicious that my judgment is cloudy and my mind is wandering. The insanity you've been waiting for is now approaching and may come at any moment. Now you have to decide whether it's better for you if I'm sane or insane. Consider! If I go mad, I will have to leave the service, and where does that leave you? If I die, you get my life insurance. If I take my life, you get nothing. It is therefore in your interest for me to live out my life.

LAURA: Are you laying a trap?

CAPTAIN: Of course! But it's up to you to avoid it or put your head in it.

LAURA: You speak of killing yourself. You'd never do that.

CAPTAIN: Don't be too sure. Do you expect a man to go on living when he has nothing and nobody to live for?

LAURA: Then you surrender?

CAPTAIN: No, I'm offering peace.

LAURA: And the conditions?

CAPTAIN: That I keep my reason. Free me from doubts and I'll give up the battle.

LAURA: What doubts?

CAPTAIN: About Bertha's parentage.

LAURA: Do you have doubts about that?

CAPTAIN: Yes, I have doubts, and it's you who created them.

LAURA: I did?

CAPTAIN: Yes. You dropped them like seeds in my ear and circumstances made them grow. Deliver me from uncertainty. Confirm my suspicions and I'll forgive you in advance.

LAURA: You can't expect me to admit to a sin I haven't committed.

CAPTAIN: Why should you care when you know I won't reveal it? Would any man announce his shame in public?

LAURA: If I tell you it's not true, you'll still be uncertain. You'll only believe me if I admit it. You must want it to be true.

CAPTAIN: Oddly enough, I do. Because the first proposition cannot be proven. Only the second can.

LAURA: Do you have any grounds for your suspicions?

CAPTAIN: Yes and no.

LAURA: I think you want to prove me guilty so you

can get rid of me and gain absolute control over the child. You won't catch me in that trap.

CAPTAIN: If I were convinced of your guilt, would I want another man's child?

LAURA: I'm sure you wouldn't, which is why you were lying just now when you said you'd forgive me in advance.

CAPTAIN: *(rising)* Laura, save me and my reason. You don't understand what I'm saying. If the child isn't mine, I have no rights over her and I won't ask for any. And that's what you want, isn't it? You'll have absolute power over the child along with my financial support.

LAURA: Power, yes. That's what this whole life and death struggle is about—power!

CAPTAIN: This child was my future existence, my immortality, the only one that's real. I don't believe in an afterlife. Take away my child and you rob me of existence.

LAURA: Why didn't we separate in time?

CAPTAIN: Because the child bound us together, but the bond became a chain. And how did that happen? How? I never thought about this before, but now the memories crowd in, filled with accusation, condemnation. We'd been married for two years but had no child. You're the one who knows why. I got sick and almost died. One day, in a fever, I heard people talking in the next room. It was you and our lawyer discussing my estate. He was saying that you couldn't inherit my property because we had no children. He asked if you were pregnant. I couldn't hear your reply. I got well and we had a child. Who is the father?

53

LAURA: You.

CAPTAIN: No, I am not. There's a crime buried here which is beginning to stink. And it's a hellish crime. You women were concerned enough about freeing the black slaves, but you kept the white ones. I have slaved for you, your child, your mother, your servants. I have sacrificed my career, my promotion. I have suffered torture, depression, insomnia for your sake until my hair has turned grey. I have endured this so that you might enjoy a life without care, and, when you grew old, enjoy it again through your child. This is the basest kind of theft, the cruelest form of slavery. I have had seventeen years of penal servitude, and I was innocent! What can you give me in return?

LAURA: Now you really are mad.

CAPTAIN: That is your hope! I watched your efforts to hide your crime, and pitied you because I didn't understand. I have soothed your conscience, thinking I was chasing away bad thoughts. I heard you crying out in your sleep and shut my ears. I remember now, the night before last—Bertha's birthday—I was up reading. It was two or three in the morning, and you let out a scream as if you were being choked: "Don't, don't." I pounded on the wall with my fist—I didn't want to hear any more. For a long time, I have been suspicious but didn't want my suspicions confirmed. This is what I have suffered for you. What will you do for me?

LAURA: What *can* I do? Swear to God and all I hold sacred that you are Bertha's father?

CAPTAIN: What use is that when you have already said that a mother is prepared to commit any

54

crime for her child? I beg you for the sake of the past, I beg you like a wounded man asks to be put out of his misery, tell me the truth. Can't you see that I'm helpless as a child? Can't you hear me calling as to a mother? Won't you forget that I am a man, a soldier who can command men and beasts? I ask your pity like a sick man. I give up my power and only pray for mercy.

LAURA: *(laying her hand on his brow)* What? You crying, and a man?

CAPTAIN: Yes, I am crying. Has not a man eyes? Has not a man hands, limbs, senses, opinions, passions? Is he not fed with the same food as a woman, hurt by the weapons, warmed and cooled by the same summer and winter? If you prick us, do we not bleed? If you tickle us, do we not laugh? And if you poison us, do we not die? Why shouldn't a man complain, a soldier cry? Because it is unmanly? Why is it unmanly?

LAURA: Weep then, my child, and you will have your mother again. Don't you remember it was as a second mother that I entered your life? Your body was strong, but your nerve was weak. You were a giant child who had come into the world too soon, perhaps unwanted.

CAPTAIN: That's true. My parents had me against their will, and so I was born without a will. That's why I thought I was completing myself when you and I were married, and that is why you dominated. I, the commander in the barracks, became the subordinate at home. I grew up by you, considered you a superior being, and listened to you like an ignorant child.

LAURA: Yes, that's so, and it was as a little child

55

that I loved you. But you must have seen how ashamed I was when your feelings changed and you came to me as a lover. The joy I felt in your arms turned to horror as if my very blood was tainted. The mother turned into the mistress. Ugh!

CAPTAIN: I saw, but didn't understand. I thought you despised me for being unmanly. I tried to win you as a woman through my potency as a man.

LAURA: That was your mistake. The mother was your friend, you see, but the woman was your enemy, and love between the sexes is strife. And don't ever think I gave myself to you. I didn't give, I took—what I wanted. But you did have an advantage over me. I knew it...and I wanted you to know it.

CAPTAIN: You always had the advantage. You could hypnotize me with my eyes wide open, so that I saw nothing, heard nothing, but only obeyed. You could give me a raw potato and make me think it was a peach. You could convince me your stupid ideas were strokes of genius. You could entice me into corrupt, dishonorable actions. You had no real intelligence, but you refused to be guided by me and always followed your own instincts. And when at last I awoke and realized I had lost my honor, I wanted to compensate with some heroic deed, some great achievement, or even an honorable suicide. I wanted to go to war, but they wouldn't let me. It was then that I plunged into scientific research. And now, when I am just about to harvest the fruits, you chop off my arm. You've taken away my laurels. My life is over. For a man cannot live without reputation.

LAURA: And a woman can?

CAPTAIN: Yes, because she has her children, which he has not. But all of us, the whole of humanity, went on living unconscious as children, full of fantasies, ideals, illusions, until we awoke and it was over. But we woke up with our feet on the pillow, and the person who waked us was a sleepwalker himself. When women get old and stop being women, they grow beards on their chins. What happens to men, I wonder, when they grow old and stop being men? Those who crowed were no longer cocks, they were capons, and only pullets answered their call. Just when we thought the sun was about to rise, we found ourselves back in full moonlight in the rubble of ancient ruins, just as in bygone times. It had been only a light morning sleep filled with transparent dreams, and there was no awakening.

LAURA: You should have been a poet, you know.

CAPTAIN: Perhaps.

LAURA: But now I'm sleepy, so if you have any more fantasies, keep them till tomorrow.

CAPTAIN: One thing more about what's real—do you hate me?

LAURA: Sometimes, when you're a man.

CAPTAIN: That's like race hatred. If it's true we come from apes, it must have been two distinct species. We're not the same at all, are we?

LAURA: What are you trying to say?

CAPTAIN: That in this battle, one of us must go under.

LAURA: Which one?

57

CAPTAIN: The weaker one, of course.

LAURA: And the stronger one will be right?

CAPTAIN: Of course, since he has the power.

LAURA: Then I am in the right.

CAPTAIN: Do you think you have the power, then?

LAURA: Yes, the legal power to have you put under restraint.

CAPTAIN: Under restraint?

LAURA: Yes, and then I shall be able to educate my child without the benefit of your fantastic ideas.

CAPTAIN: And who will pay for her education when I'm gone?

LAURA: Your pension.

CAPTAIN: *(moving towards her threateningly)* How can you have me put under restraint?

LAURA: *(producing a letter)* By means of this letter, the attested copy of which is now in the hands of the authorities.

CAPTAIN: What letter?

LAURA: *(retreating)* Your letter! Your admission to the doctor that you are insane. *(he stares at her in silence)* You have now fulfilled your regrettably necessary function as a father and a provider. You are no longer needed and you must go. You must go. You have discovered that my intellect is as strong as my will, and you don't have the strength to say, I admit it! I admit it! I admit it! *(the Captain goes to the table, takes the lighted lamp, and throws it at Laura, who escapes backwards through the door)*

58

ACT 3

The same. The following evening. A new lamp is on the table, lighted. The private door is barricaded with a chair. Pacing above. Laura and the Nurse.

LAURA: Did he give you the keys?

NURSE: Give them to me? No, God help me, I took them out of the coat Nojd was brushing.

LAURA: So it's Nojd who's on duty?

NURSE: Yes, Nojd.

LAURA: Give me the keys.

NURSE: Here—but it feels just like stealing. Listen to him up there. Back and forth, back and forth.

LAURA: Are you sure the door is safely locked?

NURSE: It's bolted. *(weeps)*

LAURA: *(opens the desk and sits down)* Control yourself, Margaret. Only clear heads can help us now. *(a knock at the hall door)* See who that is.

NURSE: *(at the door)* It's Nojd.

LAURA: Tell him to come in.

NOJD: *(entering)* Message from the Colonel.

LAURA: Give it to me. *(reads)* I see.... Nojd, have you removed the bullets from all the guns and belts?

NOJD: Just like you said, ma'am.

LAURA: Wait outside while I write an answer to the Colonel.

(Exit Nojd. Laura writes. Sound of sawing upstairs.)

NURSE: Do you hear that, madam? What is he doing up there?

LAURA: Be quiet. I'm writing.

NURSE: Merciful God, where will it all end?

LAURA: *(finishes)* Here, give this to Nojd. And tell my mother nothing, do you understand?

(Nurse exits. Laura opens the desk drawer and takes out papers. Enter Pastor.)

PASTOR: Laura, I'm just back. I hear terrible things have happened.

LAURA: Yes, brother. I've never been through such a night and such a day.

PASTOR: But you're looking all right, nevertheless.

LAURA: I am all right, thank God. But just think what might have happened.

PASTOR: Tell me about it. All I know is rumors. How did it all start?

LAURA: It began with him carrying on about not being Bertha's father, and ended with his throwing a flaming lamp in my face.

PASTOR: But that's dreadful. He must be completely insane. What must be done now?

LAURA: We must try to prevent further violence. The doctor has sent for a straitjacket. I've just written to the Colonel, and now I'm trying to make sense of our household affairs, which he has left totally botched. *(opens another drawer)*

PASTOR: It's a terrible business, but I'm not surprised. There's always an explosion when you mix fire and water. *(looks in drawer)* What is all this?

LAURA: That's where he kept everything hidden.

PASTOR: Good heavens, here's one of your old dolls. And here's your christening cap...and Bertha's old rattle...and your letters...and a locket. *(dries his eyes)* He must have loved you deeply, Laura. I never kept such things.

LAURA: I think he did love me once. But time has a way of changing things.

PASTOR: What's this document? *(examines it)* The deed for a grave plot. Well, better a grave than the lunatic asylum. Laura, tell me. Don't you feel the slightest bit of responsibility for all this?

LAURA: Am I to blame because a man goes out of his mind?

PASTOR: Well, I'll say nothing more. They say blood is thicker than water.

LAURA: And what is that supposed to mean?

PASTOR: *(gazing at her)* Oh, I think you understand.

LAURA: What?

PASTOR: Oh, come on now. You can hardly deny this puts you in full control of your daughter's future.

LAURA: I don't understand what you mean.

PASTOR: I really admire you.

LAURA: You do?

PASTOR: And it'll be my job to take charge of that Freethinker up there. You know I've always considered him a bit of a weed in our garden.

LAURA: *(suppresses a laugh)* You dare to say that to me, his wife?

PASTOR: What a will you have, Laura, how incredibly strong. You're like a fox in a trap. Rather than get caught, you'd gnaw off your leg. You're like a master thief. You won't have any accomplices, not even your own conscience. Look in your mirror! You can't.

LAURA: I never use a mirror.

PASTOR: I know. You can't look at yourself. Let me see your hand. No blood, no poison. A little innocent murder beyond the reach of the law. An unconscious crime. Unconscious. What a brilliant stroke. Listen to him up there. Be careful, Laura. If that man gets loose, he'll hack you to pieces, too.

LAURA: You sound like you're the one with a bad conscience. If you have any evidence, accuse me.

PASTOR: I can't.

LAURA: You can't. So I'm innocent. Take care of your own problem and I'll take care of mine. *(enter Doctor)* Here's the Doctor. *(rises)* I'm so relieved to see you, Doctor. I know you will help me, although there isn't very much to be done now. Can you hear him up there? Does that convince you?

DOCTOR: I am convinced an act of violence was committed, but I'm not certain whether it was caused by anger or madness.

62

PASTOR: But aside from that action, you must admit that he is rather obsessive.

DOCTOR: I suspect that you might be considered rather obsessive, too, Pastor.

PASTOR: If you're referring to my spiritual convictions...

DOCTOR: Spiritual convictions apart, it's up to you, madam, to decide whether your husband will be fined or imprisoned for violence or committed to an institution. How do you regard his behavior?

LAURA: I can't say now.

DOCTOR: Then you have no—er—spiritual convictions about what is best for your family? What's your opinion, Pastor?

PASTOR: Either way, there'll be a scandal. It's not an easy thing to decide.

LAURA: But if he only had to pay a fine, he might do the same thing again.

DOCTOR: And if he only went to prison, he'd soon be free. So it seems best for everyone that we treat this as a case of insanity. Where's the nurse?

LAURA: Why?

DOCTOR: She has to put the straitjacket on the patient. But not until I have talked to him and given the order. I have the—er—garment ready outside. *(goes to the hall and returns with a large parcel)* Please call the nurse.

(Laura rings. The Doctor begins to unpack the straitjacket.)

63

PASTOR: Dreadful! Dreadful!

(enter Nurse)

DOCTOR: Listen to me carefully. What I want you to do is slip this on the Captain from behind, but only after I decide it is necessary. We don't want any further outbreaks. As you can see, it has very long sleeves. This is to restrict his movements. You must tie these together behind his back. You see these two straps? You must fasten these with buckles to the arm of a chair or a sofa or whatever is available. Do you think you can do that?

NURSE: No, Doctor, I can't. I can't.

LAURA: Why don't you do it yourself, Doctor?

DOCTOR: Because the patient doesn't trust me. You, madam, would be the obvious one to do it, but I'm afraid he doesn't trust you either. *(Laura makes an involuntary movement)* Maybe you, Pastor ...

PASTOR: I'm afraid I must say no....

(enter Nojd)

LAURA: Did you deliver my note?

NOJD: Yes, ma'am.

DOCTOR: Oh, Nojd. You know how things are here. You know the Captain has lost his mind. You will have to help us restrain the patient.

NOJD: I'll do anything to help the Captain.

DOCTOR: You must put this jacket on him.

NURSE: He won't touch him. I won't let Nojd hurt him. I'd rather do it myself—gently, gently. Nojd

64

can stay outside and help if I need it. That's the best thing. *(loud knocking on the private door)*

DOCTOR: There he is! *(to Nurse)* Put the jacket under your shawl on the sofa. Now everyone else, get out of here. The Pastor and I will talk to him. That door won't stand up long. Hurry!

NURSE: *(exiting)* Good Lord Jesus, help us.

(Laura shuts the desk drawer and follows the Nurse. Nojd leaves, too. The door bursts open, the lock broken and the chair hurled to the floor. Enter the Captain, carrying a pile of books.)

CAPTAIN: *(putting the books on the desk)* It's all here, in every one of these books. So I'm not crazy after all. *(picks one up)* Here's *The Odyssey*, Book I, page 6, line 215 in the Uppsala version. Telemachus speaks to Athene: "My mother maintains that I am the son of Odysseus, but I cannot tell, for no man knows his own father." Telemachus can be suspicious even of Penelope, the most virtuous of women! Marvelous! No? *(another book)* The prophet Ezekiel: "The fool saith, Behold my father, but who can tell whose loins have engendered him." That's pretty clear! *(another book)* What's this one? Merzlyakov's *History of Russian Literature*. The death of Alexander Pushkin, Russia's greatest poet, was caused more by rumors of his wife's infidelity than by the bullet he received in his breast from a duel. On his deathbed he swore that she was innocent. Jackass! How could he swear? See, I know my books. Oh, Jonas, is that you? And the Doctor, naturally. Did you hear what I said to an English lady when she complained about an Irishman who threw a lighted lamp in his wife's face? "God, what women," I said. "Women," she stammered.

65

"Of course," I said. "Because when things get so bad that a man who has loved, who has worshiped, a woman has to pick up a burning lamp and throw it in her face, then you can be sure..."

PASTOR: Sure of what?

CAPTAIN: Of nothing. One can be sure of nothing. One can only have blind faith. Isn't that true, Jonas? One believes and one is saved. Wouldn't that be nice? But one can be damned through too much faith. I know that now.

DOCTOR: Listen, Captain.

CAPTAIN: Shut up! I don't want to hear any more of your shit. I don't want to hear you parroting all the gossip from in there, like a ventriloquist's dummy. In *there*! Understand? Listen, Jonas. Are you convinced you're the father of your children? I seem to remember a young tutor in your house, quite a pretty boy, too, and wasn't there a little gossip, too?

PASTOR: Stop it, Adolph.

CAPTAIN: Grope under your toupee and see if you can't find two little bumps there. My God, he's turned white. Well, it was only talk, of course, but God, what a lot of talk! Still, we married men were born to be figures of fun, everyone of us. Isn't that right, Doctor? How about your own marriage? Didn't you have a young lieutenant in the house? Now, what was his name? Let me guess. Wasn't it *(whispers in the Doctor's ear)*. By God, his complexion's turned to cheese, too. But forget about it. She's dead and gone, and what's done cannot be undone. Are you aware I knew him? He's now a—look at me, Doctor. No, straight in the eye. He's now a major in the Dragoons. By God, I think this one's got horns, too.

DOCTOR: *(angry)* I'd appreciate it if you changed the subject, Captain.

CAPTAIN: See? I mention horns, he wants to change the subject.

PASTOR: Do you know, Adolph, that your mind is sick?

CAPTAIN: I know that. But if I had your two royal heads in my hands for a while, I'd soon get you locked up, too. I am mad, but what drove me mad? Does that interest you? No, it doesn't interest anyone. *(takes the photo album from the table)* Jesus Christ, that is my child. Mine? Who can ever know that? I'll tell you how to be sure. First get married to satisfy society. Then divorce immediately and become lovers. And finally adopt the children. That way you'll at least be sure that they're your *adopted* children. Got it? But what good is that to me? What good is anything now that you've robbed me of my immortal life? What good are science and philosophy when I've nothing left to live for? How can I survive without honor? I grafted my right arm, half my brain, and half my bone marrow on to another stem, thinking they would unite into a more perfect tree. Then someone took a knife and cut below the graft, and now I'm only half a tree. The other half goes right on growing, with my one arm and half my brain, while I wither and die, because those were the best parts I gave away. Now I'm vanishing into thin air. Do what you like with me. I'm not here any more.

(The Doctor and Pastor whisper, and exit. The Captain sinks into a chair. Bertha enters.)

BERTHA: *(going to him)* Are you sick, Father?

CAPTAIN: *(the word "Father" shakes him)* Me?

BERTHA: Do you know what you did? You threw a lamp at Mother.

CAPTAIN: Did I?

BERTHA: Yes, you did. What if you hurt her?

CAPTAIN: Would that have mattered?

BERTHA: You're not my father if you talk like that.

CAPTAIN: What did you say? That I'm not your father? How do you know that? Who told you? And who is your father, then? Who?

BERTHA: Not you, anyway.

CAPTAIN: Not me again! Who, then? Who? You're very well informed. Who told you that? That I should live to hear my child tell me to my face I'm not her father. Don't you realize you're shaming your mother when you say that? Don't you understand what it says about her if it's true?

BERTHA: Don't say anything against Mother, do you hear?

CAPTAIN: No, you're all conspiring against me. You always have.

BERTHA: Father.

CAPTAIN: Don't call me that again!

BERTHA: Father, father.

CAPTAIN: *(hugging her to him)* Bertha, my dear child.

68

You *are* my child. Yes, it's so, it must be so. The rest was only sickness—riding on the wind like a plague or a fever. Look at me! Let me see my soul in your eyes. But I see her soul there, too. You have two souls. You love me with one and hate me with the other. You must love only me, and me alone. You must have only one soul or you'll have no peace, and I won't either. You must have only one mind, born of my mind. You must have only one will—mine!

BERTHA: No, no, I want to be myself.

CAPTAIN: You can't. You see, I'm a cannibal and I'm going to eat you. Your mother wanted to eat me, but she couldn't. I am Saturn who devoured his children because it was prophesied that they would devour him. To eat or be eaten—that is the question. If I don't eat you, you'll eat me— and I've seen your teeth already. *(goes to the rack)* Don't be frightened, my darling child. This won't hurt you. *(takes down a revolver)*

BERTHA: *(recoiling)* Help, Mother, help, he's going to kill me!

NURSE: *(coming in)* What are you doing, Mr. Adolph?

CAPTAIN: *(examining the revolver)* Have you taken out the bullets?

NURSE: Well, I did tidy things up a bit. But sit down and calm yourself and I'll bring them back soon. *(She takes the Captain by his arm and leads him to the chair. Then she takes out the straitjacket and goes behind the chair. Bertha slips out.)* Do you remember, Mr. Adolph, when you were my sweet little boy and I used to tuck you in at night? I would say your prayers with you: "Now

69

I lay me down to sleep." Remember? And do you remember how I used to get up at night and fetch you something to drink when you were thirsty? And how I would light the candle when you had bad dreams, and tell you little stories? Do you remember?

CAPTAIN: Keep talking, Margaret, it soothes my brain. Keep talking to me.

NURSE: I will, but you have to pay attention. Do you remember once when you took a great big knife from the kitchen to carve boats with, and I came in and had to trick you out of the knife? You were such a silly little boy that I had to fool you, because you never believed people meant anything for your good. "Give me that ugly snake," I said, "It's going to bite you." And then, you gave me the knife. *(takes the revolver from him)* And remember the time when you had to dress yourself and you didn't want to? I had to coax you and say you were going to have a golden coat and be dressed like a prince. And then I took your little green wool vest and held it up in front of you and said: "Put both arms in. Be a good little boy and sit nice and still while I button it down the back." *(putting on the jacket)* And then I said, "Get up and walk across the room like a good little boy so I can see how it fits." *(leads him to the sofa)* And then I said, "Now it's time to go to bed."

CAPTAIN: What did you say? Go to bed when I just got dressed? Goddamn it, what have you done to me? *(tries to free himself)* Treacherous woman, what diabolical cunning! Who could have guessed you to be so clever. *(lies down on the sofa)* Trussed, cropped, outwitted, prevented even from dying!

70

NURSE: Forgive me, Mr. Adolph, forgive me! I couldn't let you kill the child.

CAPTAIN: Why not? Life is hell and death is heaven, and children belong in paradise.

NURSE: What do you know of the afterlife?

CAPTAIN: It's all we do know. It's life of which we know nothing. If only I had realized that from the start.

NURSE: Humble your hard heart, Mr. Adolph, and ask God for mercy. It's not too late even now. It wasn't too late for the thief on the cross when our Savior said, "Today shalt thou be with me in paradise."

CAPTAIN: Croaking for the corpse already, old crow? *(she takes out her hymn book)* Nojd! Nojd! Are you there? *(enter Nojd)* Throw this woman out of the house. She's trying to strangle me with her hymn book. Throw her out of the window, stuff her up the chimney, just get rid of her.

NOJD: *(looking at the Nurse)* God help you, Captain, I can't do that. I can't. If it was six men...but a woman!

CAPTAIN: You can't handle one woman, eh?

NOJD: I could handle her all right. But a man can't lay hands on a woman.

CAPTAIN: What's the difference? Haven't women laid hands on me?

NOJD: Yes, but I just can't do it, Captain. It's like hitting the Pastor. It's against nature. I can't.

(Enter Laura who signals to Nojd. He leaves.)

71

CAPTAIN: Omphale! Omphale! Playing with your club while Hercules spins your wool.

LAURA: *(approaching the sofa)* Adolph, look at me. Do you think I'm your enemy?

CAPTAIN: Of course I do. I think you are all my enemies. My mother didn't want me to be born because my birth would give her pain. She was my enemy. She robbed me of nourishment and turned me into a weakling. My sister was my enemy when she made me do her bidding. The first woman I slept with was my enemy. She repaid my love with ten years of disease. My daughter became my enemy when she had to choose between us. And you, my wife, have been my most bitter enemy, because you would not give up until you robbed me of my life.

LAURA: I never intended this to happen. Not with my conscious mind. I may have had some vague wish to get rid of you—you were something troublesome. And if you see some design in what I did, maybe you're right, though it was always unconscious. I never thought about my actions. I just proceeded along the path you created. In my conscience I feel innocent before God—even if I'm not. You laid like a stone on my heart, pressing, pressing, until I had to throw off the heavy burden. Those are the facts, and if I am responsible for what has happened to you, I ask your forgiveness.

CAPTAIN: That sounds plausible enough, but what good does it do? And who is at fault? Perhaps our spiritual marriage is to blame. In the past you married a wife. Now you go into partner-ship with a business woman, or set up house with a friend, and end up betraying the partner

72

or raping the friend. And what becomes of love, healthy sensual love? It fades away and dies. And what happens to the issue of those love shares, payable to the bearer, without joint liability? Who is the holder when the crash comes? Who is the physical father of the spiritual child?

LAURA: Your suspicions about Bertha are completely unfounded.

CAPTAIN: That's what's so terrible. If there were any grounds for my suspicions, at least I would have something to hold onto, cling to. Now there are only shadows, hiding in the underbrush, which poke out their heads and smirk. It's like fighting with air, or firing blank cartridges in a trumped-up duel. Something tangible, however fatal, would have strengthened my resistance, roused me to action. But now my thoughts melt into thin air, my brain grinds like tinder before a fire....Put a pillow under my head, throw something over me. I'm cold, so terribly cold.

(Laura takes her shawl and lays it over him. Exit Nurse.)

LAURA: Let me have your hand, dear friend.

CAPTAIN: My hand? The hand you've strapped behind my back? Omphale! Omphale! But I can feel your shawl against my mouth. It is warm and soft like your flesh and it smells of vanilla, like your hair when you were young. When you were young, Laura, and we used to walk in the birch woods, through the primroses and thrushes—lovely, lovely! Think how beautiful life was then—and what it is now. You didn't want this to happen, and neither did I, but it happened just the same. Who then rules over us?

73

LAURA: God.

CAPTAIN: The God of strife, then. Or is it the Goddess now? Take away this cat that's lying on me. Take it away. *(Nurse enters with a pillow and removes the shawl)* Bring me my tunic. Throw it over me. *(the Nurse takes his tunic from a peg and spreads it over him)* Ah, my tough old lion-skin that you tried to take from me. Omphale! Omphale! Ah, you cunning female, lover of peace, contriver of disarmament. Wake, Hercules, before they rob you of your club! You would steal away our armor, too, and say it was only tinsel. No, it was iron, do you hear me, before it turned to tinsel. In the old days the smith forged the soldier's uniform, now it's sewn by needlewomen. Omphale! Omphale! Rude strength has fallen before treacherous weakness. Shame on you, damned woman, and curses on your sex. *(he rises up to spit, but falls back on the sofa)* What kind of pillow have you given me, Margaret? It's hard and cold like a stone. Come sit by me on a chair. *(she does)* Yes, like that. Can I put my head on your lap? Ah, that's good, warmer. Bend near me so I can feel your breast. Oh, how sweet to sleep on a woman's breast, mother or mistress. But best of all, a mother.

LAURA: Adolph, would you like to see your child?

CAPTAIN: My child? A man has no children. Only women have children. That's why the future belongs to them, and we die childless. "Now I lay me down to sleep. I pray the Lord my soul to keep."

NURSE: Listen, he's praying to God.

CAPTAIN: No, Margaret, just to you, to put me to

sleep. I'm tired, so very tired. Good night, Margaret, blessed among women. *(He raises himself, then with a cry falls back on the Nurse's knees. Laura calls for the Doctor who comes in with the Pastor.)*

LAURA: Doctor, Doctor, help. Help him, Doctor, if it's not too late. Look, he's not breathing.

DOCTOR: *(feeling his pulse)* It's a stroke.

PASTOR: Is he dead?

DOCTOR: No, he's in a coma. He may still recover— but in what state, we don't know.

PASTOR: "First death, then the judgment."

DOCTOR: No judgment, no accusations, no recriminations. You believe in a God who rules over human destiny. You'd better leave this to Him.

NURSE: Ah, Pastor, in his last moments, he prayed to God!

DOCTOR: *(to Laura)* Is that true?

LAURA: It is true.

DOCTOR: Then I am as helpless in understanding this as I am the cause of his illness. My skill is at an end. It's time for yours, Pastor.

LAURA: You can say nothing more at his deathbed, Doctor?

DOCTOR: I can say no more. I know no more. If anyone does, let him speak.

BERTHA: *(running in to Laura)* Mother! Mother!

LAURA: *My* child. My own child!

PASTOR: Amen.

(blackout)

ELEPHANT PAPERBACKS

Theatre and Drama
Robert Brustein, *The Theatre of Revolt,* EL407
Plays for Performance:
    Aristophanes, *Lysistrata,* EL405
    Anton Chekhov, *The Seagull,* EL407
    Georges Feydeau, *Paradise Hotel,* EL403
    Henrik Ibsen, *Ghosts,* EL401
    Henrik Ibsen, *When We Dead Awaken,* EL408
    Heinrich von Kleist, *The Prince of Homburg,* EL402
    Christopher Marlowe, *Doctor Faustus,* EL404
    August Strindberg, *The Father,* EL406

Literature and Letters
Stephen Vincent Benét, *John Brown's Body,* EL10
Philip Callow, *Son and Lover: The Young D. H. Lawrence,* EL14
James Gould Cozzens, *Castaway,* EL6
James Gould Cozzens, *Men and Brethren,* EL3
Clarence Darrow, *Verdicts Out of Court,* EL2
Floyd Dell, *Intellectual Vagabondage,* EL13
Theodore Dreiser, *Best Short Stories,* EL1
Joseph Epstein, *Ambition,* EL7
André Gide, *Madeleine,* EL8
Irving Howe, *William Faulkner,* EL15
Aldous Huxley, *Collected Short Stories,* EL17
Sinclair Lewis, *Selected Short Stories,* EL9
William L. O'Neill, ed., *Echoes of Revolt: The Masses,*
    1911–1917, EL5
Ramón J. Sender, *Seven Red Sundays,* EL11
Wilfrid Sheed, *Office Politics,* EL4
Tess Slesinger, *On Being Told That Her Second Husband Has
    Taken His First Lover, and Other Stories,* EL12
Thomas Wolfe, *The Hills Beyond,* EL16